Bumper Sticker

(the book)

Thought Provoking Sayings
to Think, Talk, and Write About

> *Faith is taking the first step*
> *even when you don't see*
> *the whole staircase.*
> *Martin Luther King, Jr*

> Isn't it strange that
> in this Age of Information
> truth is so hard to find?

Collected and edited by
Arthur A. Burrows

PRO LINGUA ● ASSOCIATES

Contents

Pro Lingua Associates, Publishers
P.O. Box 1348
Brattleboro, Vermont 05302 USA
Office: 802-257-7779; Orders: 800-366-4775
Email: info@ProLinguaAssociates.com
WebStore: www.ProLinguaAssociates.com
SAN: 216-0579

*At Pro Lingua
our objective is to foster an approach to learning and teaching that we call
interplay, the **inter**action of language learners and teachers with their materials,
with the language and culture, and with each other in active, creative,
and productive **play**.*

Copyright © 2013 by Pro Lingua Associates

ISBN 13: 978-0-86647-346-0; 10: 0-86647-346-7

The bumper stickers in this book were collected and selected by Arthur A. Burrows, and the book was designed and set by him. A great variety of type faces were used, suggesting the variety of designs used for the stickers. Art for the cover was chosen from Dreamstime.com: car © Dawn Hudson, ribbon © Beaniebeagle, Dachshund © Suto Norbert, Uncle Sam © Anna Velichkovsky. Illustrations inside, with the exceptions of the bumper above © Iurii Davydov/Dreamstime.com, the SUVs on stickers # 76 and 183 © Faberfoto/Dreamstime.com, and the toad #29 © Dannyphoto80/Dreamstime.com, are either typographic dingbats or clipart selected from The Big Book of Art 8,00,000 © 2003 Hermera Technologies.

Teachers and students are encouraged to look for sources of good Bumper Stickers. In most cases I have no way of knowing the sources of stickers in this collection, but here are a few sources to explore: zazzle.com, cafepress.com, internetbumperstickers.com, and prankplace.com. You will note that some sayings are used by more than one source; the sayings are in the public domain.

While collecting, I have noticed that a few bumper sticker creators have credited the origin of the sayings – to Einstein, for example. Sometimes while driving, we could catch these credits. Where I could, I have included this information. Because of the way they are used, all of these sayings are in the public domain. However, in some cases the *design* of the bumper sticker has been copyrighted. This is valid. I claim the copyright to this book on the same basis. In no case have I used the original design. If any of the sticker writers would like to have me credit them, I will gladly do so in a future printing should there be one. For now, thank you to all who have contributed to this book. And may everyone, student and teacher, enjoy it as much as I have.

Printed in the United States of America
First printing 2013.

Preface

BUMPER STICKERS have been a North American cultural phenomenon since the 1930's, soon after the bumper was invented and added to the Model A Ford. Since then they have been popular in the United States and Canada. They are also seen in other countries, but the bumper sticker sayings collected in this book are from North America. In many ways, they offer insights into the thinking, personality, and humor of the diverse people of our two nations.

Ray Clark, our editor and partner in Pro Lingua, came up with the idea of collecting bumper stickers to use as prompts for discussion in ESL classrooms. He was the prime mover on this fun project, and he started me and several friends collecting. Elise Burrows, Mike Jerald, David and Peggy Kehe, Ace Hood, and Sarah Egerer contributed finds. In 2007, after we had enough, we added a page of these sayings to our master resource, *The ESL Miscellany*. Since then I have continued collecting as I have traveled around the country with the idea of putting this book together.

I collected all kinds of sayings. One of the contributors to the Wikipedia "Bumper Stickers" article summarized the range of sayings this way: "Bumper stickers can be commercial, religious, secular, humorous, or in support of a sports team or other organization. They may promote or oppose a particular philosophical or political position. In some countries, such as the United States, bumper stickers are a popular way of showing support for a candidate for a government seat and become more common during election years." In putting this book together, I selected sayings in the secular, humorous, and philosphical range, thought provoking sayings that give the reader something to think, talk, and write about. I also looked for wit, slang, and idiomatic language.

Following this preface, I have included a brief introduction to bumper stickers for readers from other cultures. You may photocopy this, hand it out to your students, and discuss it, as a way of explaining the stickers in general and of putting this collection in context.

Ray Clark has once again become excited by the teaching potential of these bumper stickers as prompts for language practice, and he has kindly added a user's guide of fourteen techniques to engage your students in activities that will strengthen many of their language skills. Ray also developed a Bumper Sticker Index, which will help you find sayings on a specific topic, for example, Peace/War or Family.

A. A. Burrows

Introduction:

*Why do so many People in the U.S. and Canada
Love Bumper Stickers?*

It is very strange that we North Americans like to put bumper stickers on our cars for anyone and everyone to see. As a general rule, we keep our opinions to ourselves. Some of us boast loudly of our accomplishments and like to argue our opinions with anyone who will listen, but most of us don't. We generally try to avoid saying anything provocative in public. We try to get along even when we disagree. However, ironically, we delight in boasting and expressing opinions of all sorts on the outside of our cars. The sayings we paste on our cars, called bumper stickers, are usually very brief and often witty, clever and funny.

Expressing ourselves with bumper stickers goes in and out of fashion. Sometimes they are super popular in Colorado, sometimes in Calgary, sometimes in Connecticut. During political campaigns, we see lots of bumper stickers, usually with a politician's name and the office she or he is running for – they sometimes use only their first name or their family name. These stickers are sometimes simple – the driver is saying, I want "Marco Rubio for President." You will notice that often the sticker doesn't say which political party the candidate belongs to. Sometimes the wording or the design of the sticker is clever. On one witty example, Bernie Sanders says he is running "for *us*," all the people of his state, and "for the *U.S. Senate.*" It says simply:

BERNIE for US SENATE

We use bumper stickers to make many different kinds of statements in public. Travelers often decorate their cars with stickers showing what cities, states/provinces they have visited; sometimes they use stickers to say where they come from. "Not only am I perfect, I'm Canadian!" Internationally cars often have small oval decals/stickers indicating what country they come from with either an abbreviation of the country name or a symbol – "D" for Germany or a maple leaf for Canada. In the U.S. we use the state abbreviations – "CA" for California. Sometimes we use these ovals for other messages – "VPR" for Vermont Public Radio. Other travelers' stickers have slogans like "Virginia is for Lovers," or "I ♥ NY." Travelers also like to announce where they're going – "Disney World or Bust," or where they have been "I Climbed Mt. Wachusett," "The Paddlewheeler CREOLE QUEEN, Port of New Orleans," "Remember the Alamo," and "We won't forget Wounded Knee."

Stickers promoting favorite bands, events, restaurants, resorts, etc., are often colorful and fun: "*South by Southwest* in Austin," "The Grateful Dead Forever," "Willie Nelson Live at *Grand Ole Opry*, Nashville," "Adele at Royal Oak," "Herbie's Crab Shack," "Ghirardelli Chocolate on the Embarcadero, San Francisco," "Blue Water Cafe and Raw Bar, Vancouver, BC," "Wisconsin Dells," "Graceland," "Ben & Jerry's Factory Tour," "Don't Miss Niagara Falls," and "Grand Canyon Dreamin'!"

Another type of bumper sticker uses pictures rather than words. The picture may show a specific breed of cat or dog. A circle with a bar through it means that the driver opposes what is pictured in the circle; it might be an automatic weapon or the mushroom cloud of an atomic explosion. Other symbols show the drivers interest in specific sports and products.

Sometime stickers use symbols and words. A sticker with a flag or shield may say, "U.S. Marine - Retired" or "Support Our Troops." A sticker with a picture of a snowflake may say, "Think Snow!" A picture of a loop of colored ribbon means "remember." There are many kinds of issues we are not to forget: the search for a cure for breast cancer and for HIV, or our troops overseas, or MIAs (missing in action).

Collecting all kinds of bumber stickers is a fun way to "explore" North American geogrpahy and culture. Ask questions about your stickers. Ask anyone. Ask lots of people, young and old, friends and strangers. Find out where the stickers come from and what they mean, and you'll get conflicting opinions. Google. You will learn a lot about North American geography, history, and culture.

Part of the fun in collecting is to imagine what kind of person put the stickers on their car and why. Explain to someone else what you think the driver might be like, and ask their opinion. Talk about both the driver and the stickers. You'll find your friends will have lots of different ideas and insights to share.

The stickers in this book are not about politicians. They are not about interesting places to visit. This is a collection of bumper stickers that express people's opinions on a great variety of subjects from religion to politics to the environment to the "battle of the sexes." Most use humor and witty language. Both the bumper stickers and this book are meant to prompt you to think and talk. "What could this mean?" "Could this possibly be true?" "Who would put such a bumper sticker on their car, and why?

How is the book organized? When you go collecting bumper stickers as I have, you find them higgledy-piggledy, all mixed up. That is part of the fun. Sometimes on the same car there are very different kinds of sayings. So that is how this book is organized, all higgledy-piggledy, full of fun surprises. Enjoy my collection.

Honk if you love silence.

1

*Every mother is
a working mother.*

2

SPLIT WOOD NOT ATOMS

3

Well behaved women
rarely make history.

4

I started with nothing
and have most of it left.

5

Goin Solar?

6

We are not human beings having a spiritual experience.
We are spiritual beings having a human experience.

7

**Someone you know
may need a choice.**

8

Your vote is your voice.

9

10

*Think globally.
Eat neighborly.*

11

It's time for trains.

12

Still Pro-nuclear?
Get a half-life!

13

Make art, not war.

14

*One people. One planet.
One future.*

15

No farms. No food.

16

In a time of universal deceit,
telling the truth is a revolutionary act.

17

THREE THINGS CANNOT LONG BE HIDDEN:
THE SUN, THE MOON, AND THE TRUTH. BUDDHA

18

Good planets
are hard to find.

19

THAT WAS ZEN.
THIS IS TAO.

20

My job is to comfort the disturbed
and disturb the comfortable. Cesar A. Cruz

21

Peace cannot be kept by force.
It can only be achieved by understanding.
Albert Einstein

22

THE MORE YOU KNOW
THE LESS YOU NEED.
An aboriginal saying

23

You cannot simultaneously
prevent and prepare for war.
Albert Einstein

24

Work is for people
who don't fish.

25

IF it is nothing,
why do it?

26

Kids in sports
stay out of courts.

27

Failure is impossible.

Susan B. Anthony

28

Witch wagon
Tailgaters will be toad  !

29

Happy childhoods last a lifetime.
Prevent child abuse.

30

If you can read this,
you're too damned close.

31

Erase Hate.

32

My dog is smarter than
your honor student.

33

Fight TV addiction.

34

Don't treat your soil like dirt.

35

Sow justice. Reap peace.

36

I owe, I owe,
it's off to work I go!

37

Celebrate Diversity.

38

Eat Bertha's mussels.

39

Those who vote decide nothing.
Those who count the votes
decide everything. Stalin

40

Ignore your rights,
and they'll go away.

41

Real women drive trucks.

42

It's never OK to hit a child.

43

School's open. Drive carefully.

44

Two's company.
3, 6, 9 billion's a crowd.

45

Earth Lover.

46

For your health, eat organic.

47

Never trust a skinny cook.

48

Hands off Indian land.

49

Visualize
using your turn signal.

50

My wife, yes. My dog, maybe.
My gun, **never**.

51

Learning is natural.
Education is optional.

52

There is no flag big enough
to cover the shame
of killing innocent people.

53

God gave us two ears and one mouth,
so we should listen twice as much as we speak.

An Hadith of the Prophet

54

No one is free
when others are oppressed.

55

Hatred is not a family value.

56

Wage peace.

57

Legalize skateboarding.

58

Habitat loss = Species loss
= Our loss.

59

Your kids are watching.

60

What is a weed? A plant whose virtue is yet to be discovered. *Emerson*

61

Aging is the only way to live.

62

Why worry? God's in control.

63

The future belongs to those who give the next generation reason for hope.
Pierre Teilhard de Chardin

64

*The labor movement,
the folks who brought you into the world.*

65

She who laughs, lasts.

66

What would Buddha do?

67

Grow slow.

68

Brake for moose.
It could save your life.

69

You say I'm a dreamer,
but I'm not the only one. John Lennon

70

Ignorance and arrogance
is a bad foreign policy.

71

Honk if you love cheeses.

Wisconsin, The Dairy State

72

*Local food,
thousands of miles fresher.*

73

We must be the change we
wish to see in the world. Gandhi

74

Stop bitching.
Start a revolution.

75

I love asphalt.

76

Do not meddle in the affairs of Dragons, for
you are crunchy and good with ketchup.

77

Change is inevitable.
Growth is optional.

78

Not all who wander are lost.

79

Just let go.

80

*A woman's place
is in control.*

81

POWER TO THE PEACEFUL.

82

If you object to logging,
try using plastic toilet paper.

83

"Catch the Buzz."
Keep bees.

84

Graze.

85

PICTURE A MAN WITH A DRUM.
IT'S AN INDIAN THING. YOU
WOULDN'T UNDERSTAND.

86

*… and what difference
do you make?*

87

Compost happens.

88

Dogs are family. Would you chain
your grandma outside?

89

Do no harm.

90

I think, THEREFORE
I'm dangerous.

91

If only closed minds
came with closed mouths.

92

Those who make you believe absurdities,
can make you commit atrocities.
Voltaire

93

It is easier to raise strong children
than to repair broken men. *Frederick Douglas*

94

Books not bombs.

95

WAG MORE.
bark less.

96

Simplify.

97

Farm land lost
is farmland lost forever.

98

Cukes not nukes.

99

May the forest be with you.

100

Haiku confuse me
Too often they make no sense
Hand me the pliers

101

Respect for women
creates good karma.

102

None are more hopelessly enslaved,
than those who falsely believe they are free. *Goethe*

103

"It is not our differences that divide us,
it's our inability to recognize, accept, and
celebrate those differences." – *Andre Lorde*

104

 Peace through music.

105

 *The one and Only.*

106

Darwin lives.

107

Remember you're UNIQUE,
like everyone else.

108

Live simply
that others may simply live.

109

ENLIGHTEN UP.

110

War is costly. Peace is priceless.

111

Politicians and diapers need to be
changed – often for the same reason.

112

*Better to build school rooms for boys
than prisons for men.*

113

Plant seeds & sing songs.

114

An eye for an eye
leaves the whole world blind.

115

Keep your temper.
No one else wants it.

116

Clarity of thought. Warmth of heart.
Strength of purpose.

117

The best way to predict the future
is to help create it.

118

***Don't believe everything
you think.***

119

Those who are truly educated
never graduate.

120

Fertilize your mind.

121

Information is power.

122

I'm for the separation of church and hate.

123

A day without fairies is a day without sunshine.

124

KEEP YOUR LAWS OFF MY BODY.

125

Renewable energy is *homeland security*.

126

STOP FACTORY FARMING.

127

It don't matter to Jesus.

128

It doesn't take many words to speak the truth. Chief Joseph

129

Crunchy flakes or red meat? Eat right! Vote Republican!

130

I believe in dragons, good men, and other fantasy creatures.

131

THE PRICE OF APATHY IS TO BE RULED BY EVIL MEN   PLATO

132

I brew the beer I drink.

133

It's no meaure of good health to be well-adjusted to a sick society. Krishna Murti

134

The more slowly trees grow at first, the sounder they are at the core, and I think the same is true of humans. Henry David Thoreau

135

I don't do mornings.

136

When the power of love overcomes the love of power, the world will know peace.

137

War is the real enemy.

138

Whatever you do may seem insignificant,
but it is most important that you do it.

Gandhi

139

Value diversity.

140

Confucius say: *War is not won by those who are right but by those who are left.*

141

Stop hate crimes.
Honor diversity!

142

Human milk
for human babies.

143

*It'll be a great day when our schools have
all the $ they need, and the Pentagon has to get its budget
approved by the voters!*

144

Once you've hugged a logger, you'll never go back to trees.

145

In search of the Eternal Buzz.

146

Why be normal?

147

Trees are the answer.

148

It's too bad that the people who know how to run the country are teaching school.

149

Subvert the Dominant Paradigm.

150

I'd rather b hay'n.

151

Stay human.

152

I'm thinking the same thing about you.

153

Who died and made you
Darth Vader?

154

Vizualize
free parking.

155

Just visiting this planet.

156

Pursue insanity.

157

I'd rather be playing
Ultimate *Frisbee*.

158

Commit random acts of kindness
and senseless beauty.

159

Minds are like parachutes.
They only function when open.

160

Something wonderful is
about to happen.

161

 Lord help me to be the man
my dog thinks I am.

162

Real men wear makeup.

163

If the people lead,
the leaders will follow.

164

Imagination is more important
than knowledge.

165

Last time we mixed politics with religion,
people got burned at the stake.

166

Doing my part to piss off
the radical right.

167

Groove matters.

168

Proud parent of
a D.A.R.E. graduate

169

Humans are not the only creatures on Earth.
We just act like it.

170

DARWIN LOVES YOU.

171

Kids learn what they live.
Stop violence everywhere!

172

I'm not speeding.
I'm qualifying.

173

The Labor Movement:
the folks who brought you the weekend!

174

Allow prejudice to grow,
and violence will follow.

175

The problems we face will not be solved
by the minds that created them.

176

Revolution is a lifestyle,
not a war.

177

Justice without Revenge.

178

BACK OFF!
I'M A GODDESS!

170

If you're not outraged,
you're not paying attention.

180

Keep the fish.
Throw the old lady back.

181

 Back by popular demand.

182

Answer my prayer:
steal this car.

183

Find what you love.
Love what you find.

184

It's easier to make a baby
than raise a child.

185

One nation.
MANY FAITHS.

186

A terrorist is a freedom fighter who attacks you.
A freedom fighter is a terrorist who attacks somebody else.

187

WHICH TRIBE OWNS THE WALL STREET CASINO?

188

When you invite people to think, you are inviting revolution. Ivone Gebara

189

We don't want a piece of the pie.
We want a different pie. *Winona LaDuke*

190

World peace begins at home.

191

We all live downstream.

192

 • **35**

Earth matters.
Go green.

193

I vant to be alone. Greta Garbo

194

Where have all the hippies gone?

195

What's popular is not always right.
What's right is not always popular.

196

We don't have a democracy.
We have an auction.

197

Uppity Women,
unite and dance!

198

No Justice/No Peace
Know Justice/ Know Peace

199

You measure democracy by the freedom it gives its
dissidents, not the freedom it gives
its assimilated conformists. Abbie Hoffman

200

A woman without a man
is like a fish without a bicycle.

201

Why are we banning toy guns
and keeping the real ones???

202

My other car is a classic
Mustang!

203

Warning. *I break for animals!*

204

There is no way to Peace.
Peace is the way.

205

If you haven't changed your mind lately,
how do you know you still have one?

206

Bread, not bombs!

207

208

There is no violent solution.

209

5% of the world's people consume a third of its resources
& make nearly half of its waste. That 5% is US.

210

Believing bullshit
won't make it come true.

211

*Earth can no longer afford
the rich.*

212

Dog is my co-pilot.

213

Eracism,
all colors with love and respect.

214

Question assumptions.

215

Hate **has no home here!**

216

War = Terror

217

Love makes a family.

218

If you think the system is working,
ask someone who isn't.

219

If every vote counts,
count every vote.

220

Better a bleeding heart
than none at all.

221

The most violent element in society
is ignorance.

222

Morality matters.
Character counts.

223

If I wanted to listen to the crap coming out of your radio,
I'd be sitting in your car!

224

 EXTINCT IS FOREVER!

225

FEMINISM is the radical notion
that women are people.

226

Fearful people
do foolish things.

227

228

I dig gardens.

229

UNDO RACISM.

230

In the end, the human race
will die of too much civilizaton.

231

Don't postpone joy.

232

Don't tell the truth.
You might lose your funding.

233

Don't assume I share
your prejudices.

234

Why do you trust
corporate media?

235

Deforestation.
Doorway to hell.

236

Want a taste of religion?
Lick a witch.

237

I  Dorks.

238

Visualize
Whirled Peas.

239

Bagpipes spoken here.

240

 • **43**

If guns are outlawed, only outlaws will shoot their kids accidentally.

241

Invest in America.
Buy a Congressman.

242

It's a scientific fact:
scum always rises to the top.

243

 **Indian Country.**

244

Insatiable, not sustainable.

245

Buckle Up!
Click it, or Ticket.  **It's the Law!**

246

Bumper Sticker

If you 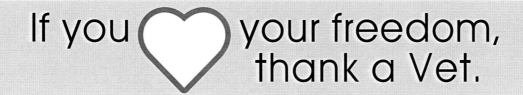 your freedom, thank a Vet.

247

Why do we kill people who kill people to show that killing people is wrong?

248

I'm here in person.

249

I don't quit 'til the last dance.

250

Enough is enough!
Neuter your pets!

251

The whole world is going to hell,

and I'm driving the bus.

252

Farms, not arms.

253

Tree hugging dirt worshipper.

254

The only constant is change.
Evolution is.

255

*If you're born again,
do you have two bellybuttons?*

256

Hang up and drive.

257

How can this be a free country
if everything is for sale?

258

Driver carries no cash –
all spent on the horse.

259

Age is an issue of mind over matter.
If you don't mind, it doesn't matter. Mark Twain

260

The hole in the ozone
is related to the hole in your head.

261

If there is no struggle,
there is no progress. Frederick Douglas

262

If we don't change direction,
we'll end up where we're going.

263

I defeat my enemies
when I make many friends.

264

 *Love your mother.*

265

"Maximize shareholder values."
A natural law.

266

Being a self-sufficient, well-adjusted adult is highly overrated.

267

**Change how you see,
not how you look.**

268

*Once is not enough.
Recycle.*

269

Our factories are all overseas!!
All we produce here are rich executives.

270

**One solution comes up
every morning.**

271

OLD KING COAL.
Past or Future?

272

Peace begins
when the hungry are fed.

273

Texas Native

274

Encourage your hopes
not your fears.

275

If ignorance is bliss,
why aren't more people happy?

276

What if the hokey pokey
is what it's all about?

277

People never lie so much as
after fishing, during a war, or before an election.

278

Racism, the affliction.
Education, the prescription.
Knowledge, the cure.

279

RECOVERING TELE-HOLIC.
BEWARE THE MEDIA TRIVIA COMPLEX.

280

Speak your mind, even if
your voice shakes. Maggie Kuhn

281

Killing one person is murder.
Killing 1000s is foreign policy.

282

God bless the whole world
without exceptions.

283

Success is easy. Rise early.
Work hard. Strike oil. *J. Paul Getty*

284

BE KIND TO ANIMALS.
DON'T EAT THEM.

285

I'm proud of my cub scout!

286

Real men love Jesus.

287

Honk if you love God.

288

 • **51**

The Big Bang. God said, "Let there be" and BANG, there was.

289

TODAY'S MIGHTY OAK IS JUST YESTERDAY'S NUT.

290

What part of *"Thou shalt not kill"* didn't you understand? *God*

291

Why encourage violence? Don't buy war toys.

292

Who would Jesus bomb?

293

WHEN RELIGION RULED THE WORLD, THEY CALLED IT THE DARK AGES.

294

"Vegetarian," the Indian name
for a lousy hunter.

295

Man does not weave the web of life.
He is merely a strand of it.
What he does to it, he does to himself.

296

Yesterday's technology,
Today's retro music.

297

If you think education is expensive,
try ignorance.

298

If we kill the innocent,
we become the enemy.

299

A patriot must be ready to protect his country
against his government.

300

Question internal combustion.

301

Urban sprawl: cut down all the trees and name streets after them.

302

Women are great leaders.
You're following one.

303

Kiss me, I'm organic.

304

Begin within.

305

The meaning of life
is to live it.

306

Labor creates all wealth.

307

The leading cause of stress
is reality.

308

It's become appallingly clear
that our technology has surpassed
our humanity. *Albert Einstein*

309

I'm straight
but not narrow.

310

Men *can* stop rape.

311

Caution: Never fly faster
than your angels can fly.

312

Love your enemies,
it really gets them confused.

313

Born again,
and again and again and again...

314

I believe in life before death.

315

Lottery: *a tax on people*
who can't do math.

316

If you surrender to hate,
you're already lost.

317

Ignorance is no excuse
for your behavior.

318

Keep your butt in your car. Earth's not your ashtray.

319

Live your own myth.

320

They're not hot flashes. They're power surges.

321

Think big thoughts, BUT
Relish small pleasures.

322

How many roads must a man travel down before he admits he is lost?

323

It's not as bad as you think, and they are out to get you.

324

I love my country, but I think we should start seeing other people.

325

Toxic pollution makes us all endangered species.

326

Those who ignore Nature are condemned to deplete it.

327

Those who abandon their dreams will discourage yours.

328

Terrorism is a sympton, not a disease.

329

Praise the children, and they will blossom.

330

*The Arts
are not a luxury.*

331

**Go to Heaven for the climate,
Hell for the company.** Mark Twain

332

Allow prejudice to grow,
and violence will follow.

333

As you sow, so shall you reap.

334

**After the last fish has been caught,
only then will you find that many can't be eaten.**
A Cree Nation prophacy

335

Diplomacy is the art of saying "Nice Doggie"
until you find a rock. **Will Rogers**

336

Forsake inhibitions.
Pursue thy dreams.

337

Everyone does better
when everyone does better.

338

Control your destiny
or someone else will.

339

Emancipate yourself from mental slavery.
None but ourselves can free our minds.
Bob Marley

340

Against abortions?
Don't have one.

341

Test peace not missiles.

342

If you can't trust me with a choice,
how can you trust me with a baby?

343

FRODO FAILED.
THE RING'S IN D.C.

344

Don't obey.

345

The best things in life
aren't things.

346

Nobody's perfect.
I'm nobody.

347

RAISED IN THE WILD
BY FOREST SPRITES AND FAIRIES.

348

My Karma ran over my Dogma.

349

Racial profiling: Guilty
until proven innocent.

350

Growth for the sake of growth is
the ideology of the cancer cell.

351

Corporations can lie.

352

KILL YOUR TELEVISION.

353

If guns are outlawed, only outlaws
will have guns.

354

Look busy. The End is at hand!

355

All men are animals.
Some just make better pets.

356

So God looked at all of Canada, and said,
"Damn, I'm good, eh?"

357

If money is the root of all evil,
why do churches beg for it?

358

Who needs terrorists? We're destroying
ourselves just fine without them.

359

Eat American lamb.
10,000 coyotes can't be wrong.

360

Your Bumper Stickers

Your Bumper Stickers

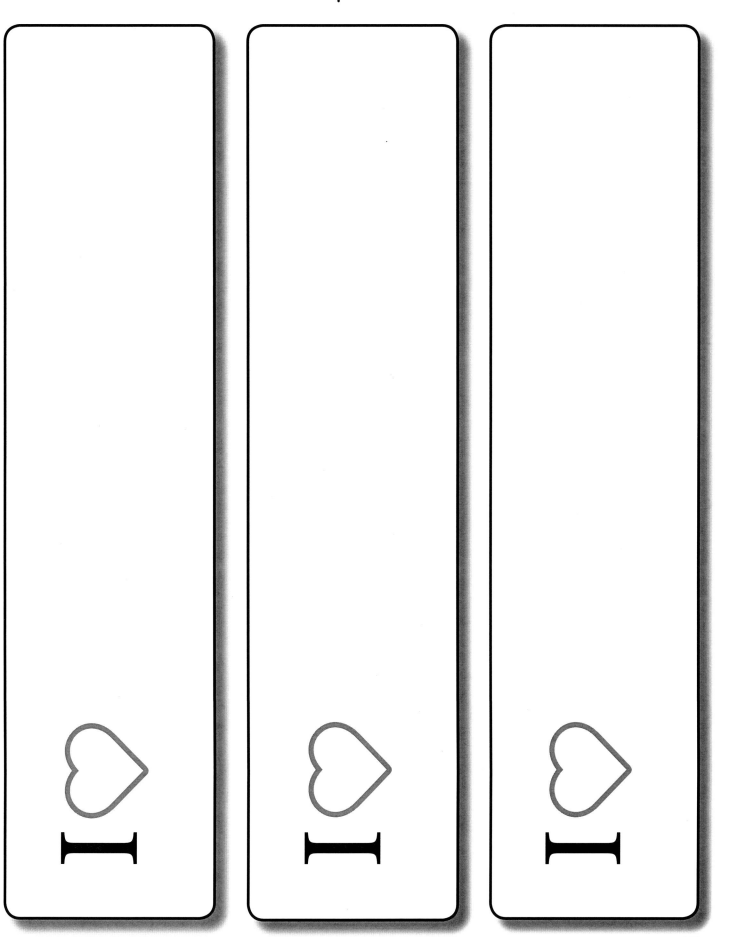

•

Bumper Sticker Users Guide
14 Teaching Techniques

I had no idea that my friend and colleague, Andy Burrows, was busily collecting bumper stickers until I found an almost completed manuscript sitting on my desk. I think I said something like, "That's quite a collection, but what do you do with it?"

Within a few minutes, the two of us had a piece of paper full of scribbled thoughts on how 350 or so "bumper stickers" were yet another kind of "Conversation Inspirations," the title of one of our more popular books, on conversation prompts. Some, of course, were not more than a chuckle that a class could have fun with for a minute or so. Some were provocative, resulting in a heated discussion or argument, and some offered insights or clues into what makes Americans tick.

This collection of bumper stickers is, essentially, 363 prompts for conversation, discussion, writing, and exploration of American society and culture. How you use them is up to you, but some suggestions may be helpful, so here are our tips on how bumper stickers can, with just a few words, enhance the language learning and teaching experience. *Ray Clark*

One-A-Day. On a regular basis, select a bumper sticker prompt, to use as a warm-up or as a closer.

1. Give everyone a copy of a sticker for the ensuing activity and for their notebook or journal.
2. Explore the meaning – first the denoted meanings of unusual vocabulary such as "half-life" or "split wood."
3. Then discuss the meaning of the entire sticker and its connotation. What is this person saying? Why are they saying it?
4. Have pairs or small groups engage in conversation. What's your reaction to this sticker? Positive? Negative? Neutral? Do you agree with this sticker? Would you give it a "like?" Give a time limit.
5. Pairs/small groups report their conversations to the rest of the class. Discuss differences and similarities.

Once-In-A-While. The procedure described above can also be used for this approach.

Simply use the technique on an occasional basis for a change of pace or just for fun. Or, select a bumper sticker that relates to the content/topic of your regular lesson, using it as a warm-up or follow-up.

Search and Collect. Choose and copy 6-8 pages at random.

1. Post the pages on the wall.
2. Give the students a topic, for example: "the environment" (See the index for a list of topics)
3. Have the students walk around with a notebook and find and write down bumper stickers that relate to the topic. Give a time limit.
4. Have the students return to their seats, and form pairs or small groups.
5. The students compare their lists and discuss similarities and differences and why they think the items on their list relate to the topic.

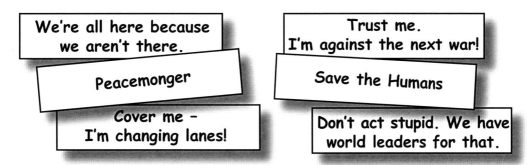

What do I say? A bumper sticker is pasted to each student's back.

1. Copy a different bumper sticker for each student.

2. *(optional)* Read the stickers one at a time with the students listening. They may not take notes. This will make the remainder of the activity a little easier.

3. Have the students come to the front of the class one at a time. Tape a bumper sticker to their backs. Be sure they don't see the sticker.

4. Have the students wander around in "a mingle." They ask each other "What do I say?" The person who is asked can look at the bumper sticker, but may not say the sentence/phrase. They have to paraphrase the sticker or explain it . For example, "It's about work and fishing. Give a time limit.

5. When the time is up, have the students try to say what they think is on their backs. Then discuss the meaning.

Fill in the Blanks. A game similar to *Wheel of Fortune*

1. Select a bumper sticker that has about 20 letters.

2. Draw a line on the board for each of the letters with gaps denoting spaces between words. For example:

__ __ __ __ __ __ __ __ __   __ __ __ __ __ __ __ __ __
(C E L E B R A T E   D I V E R S I T Y)

3. In teams, the students ask for a letter. If the sticker contains the letter, you fill it in. For example:

Team 1: Please give us the Es.

__ E __ E __ __ __ __ E   __ __ __ E __ __ __ __ __

Team 2: We'd like all the Is.

__ E __ E __ __ __ __ E   __ I __ E __ __ I __ __ __

Team 3: May we have any Ts.

__ E __ E __ __ __ T E   __ I __ E __ __ I __ T __

4. The game finishes when one team tries to guess the answer and is correct.

The Interviewer. One student "interviews" another.

1. Select 4 or 5 stickers that express an arguable opinion.

2. *(optional)* Read the stickers aloud. Check to be sure that everyone understands the stickers.

3. Pair the students and have one student be the interviewer and the other the interviewee.

4. Give each interviewer one of the stickers. Or give them two, to choose one from.

5. The interviewers conduct the interview, asking the interviewee's opinion of the sticker. Give a time limit.

6. The interviewers then report to the rest of the class what their interviewee said.

7. An alternative is to have a pair come to the front of the room and carry out the interview while the "audience" listens. Then open it up to questions from the "audience."

Write It Up. As an alternative to speaking and listening practice, have the students express their reactions/opinions in writing.

1. Choose a sticker that expresses an arguable opinion.

2. Give everyone a copy and check to be sure they understand it.

3. Ask them to write their opinion stating why they agree or disagree with the sticker.

4. Give a time limit and ask for volunteers to read their response. Or, collect the responses and read a few aloud without naming the writer.

5. Discuss the responses or ask the class to guess who wrote them.

Write One. The students create their own bumper sticker.

1. On page 64 there are blank bumper stickers you may photocopy.

2. Copy and hand out the page.

3. Ask each student to create their own bumper sticker and write it on one of the blank stickers.

4. Put the students into groups of up to six and have them dictate their stickers to each other and discuss what they mean.

5. Collect, copy, and post the students' stickers.

Color it. The students create and color a "I ♡ ..." sticker.

1. On page 65 there are three photocopyable "I ♡ ..." stickers with the object left blank.

2. Give the page to each student, and have them create one "I ♡ ..." sticker.

3. Have color markers available and ask the student to color and/or decorate their stickers.

4. Groups of three can then compare and discuss their stickers. In addition to explaining why they created the sticker, have them explain why they chose the colors they did.

Find One. A homework assignment.

1. Tell the students to look for and write down a real bumper sticker.

2. In class, the students tell and/or show what they found and what it means.

3. For additional discussion, have them note the kind of car, the driver, and other stickers on the car.

Search the Internet. Google "Bumper Sticker." There are plenty of sites.

1. Ask the students to search for ready-made bumper stickers.
2. Have them select one and bring it to class for discussion.

Make a Class Sticker.

1. There are several sites where a real sticker can be created and printed for a reasonable price. One is www.vistaprint.com.
2. Have the class discuss inventing a class sticker for a cause or for a motto or just for fun.
3. Have a competition among small groups to design a sticker.
4. Vote on a winner and have it printed.

Debate It.

1. Carry out a four-person debate (teams of two) on a bumper sticker topic.
2. Assign the topic on one day, and have the teams prepare.
3. Have the debates while the rest of the class listens.
4. If it goes well, try one debate a day until all have debated.

Impromptu. Pick a sticker from the hat.

1. Select a number of stickers that can provoke at least a half-minute impromptu "spiel."
2. Have each student, one at a time, or one a day, come to the front of the class and pull a bumper sticker out of the "hat." They have to speak for at least 30 seconds on what it means to them and whether they "buy" it or not.

I can't resist adding three more for you to use:

We could have saved the Earth, but we were too damned cheap. Kurt Vonnegut

361

War is like smoking, so easy to start, so hard to quit.

362

Sometimes I Wake up Grumpy in the Morning! Other times I let him sleep in.

363

Note: Stickers may appear in more than one category.

For more conversation, writing, and game materials, please visit us at
www.ProLinguaAssociates.com
or call our hotline 800-366-4775